G000140127

girlfriends
are forever

girlfriends are forever

Stories of Friendship

CARMEN RENEE BERRY
AND TAMARA TRAEDER

**Andrews McMeel
Publishing**

Kansas City

www.andrewsmcmeel.com
ISBN: 0-8362-5420-1
Library of Congress Catalog Card Number: 97-81430
Book design by Susan Hood

The text of this book was previously published in *girlfriends* by Carmen Renee Berry and Tamara C. Traeder
(Wildcat Canyon Press, 1995).

Silences make the real conversations between friends. Not the saying but the never needing to say is what counts.

—MARGARET LEE RUNBECK

Savoring Friendship

LOVE IS LIKE THE WILD ROSE-
    BRIAR;
FRIENDSHIP LIKE THE HOLLY-TREE.
THE HOLLY IS DARK WHEN THE
    ROSE-BRIAR BLOOMS,
BUT WHICH WILL BLOOM MOST
    CONSTANTLY?

—Emily Brontë (1846)

The most rewarding aspect of friendship is
that day-to-day (or decade-to-decade) presence, whether it be immediate or distant. As
friendships deepen and mature, we can take
comfort that our girlfriends appreciate our

support and are not offended by our bad moods or scared by our tears. We can settle into the friendship as into old slippers—remembering, of course, not to take even old slippers for granted. The dozens of women we interviewed spoke of their appreciation for and enjoyment of the following aspects of their friendships.

Loyalty

A FRIEND DOESN'T GO ON A DIET BE-
CAUSE YOU ARE FAT. A FRIEND NEVER
DEFENDS A HUSBAND WHO GETS HIS
WIFE AN ELECTRIC SKILLET FOR HER
BIRTHDAY. A FRIEND WILL TELL YOU
SHE SAW YOUR OLD BOYFRIEND—AND
HE'S A PRIEST.

—*Erma Bombeck*

There's nothing that warms the heart more
than knowing you have a loyal friend, someone who will stand by you no matter what. A
friend will defend you when you can't
defend yourself. What an honor to know that

this woman will stand up to tell the truth (or a lie, if necessary) to protect you, as illustrated by the loyalty shown by Jean to Rebecca.

Jean, now a corporate executive on the East Coast, fixed her friend Rebecca up with David—good-looking, intelligent, seemingly sweet, and a member of a prominent family—who, as Rebecca later found out, was convinced that the women in his past each viewed him as the perfect catch that got away. Ten years after David and Rebecca ended their relationship, David and Jean ran into each other, and he alluded to the fond notion that Rebecca would probably never recover from losing him. Jean, a true friend, responded, "Actually, David, I think Rebecca views you as one of a series of men she dated for a period in her life and now questions why she did it." His eyes opened wide, and he was stunned into silence. Thank goodness for loyal girlfriends like this!

A loyal friend may stand up *for* us by standing up *to* us. Katherine, a writer and editor, acknowledged that as a child she was put down, not by other kids but by herself. She told us, "I thought I was being funny by putting myself down. But I remember my friend Judy pulling me aside one time and saying, 'You know, it's not funny anymore.' And hearing it from her made me lighten up on constantly using myself as a butt of jokes."

Sometimes loyalty takes the form of supporting a friend as she sorts out what is best for her in another relationship. True girlfriends have an extraordinary ability to support us even as our situations evolve and change. Carey, a professional mediator, told us about her friend. "Ginna helped me get out of a painful marriage. She knew me

and my husband, and she managed to be friendly to him, even though he was not a particularly nice person. She frequently stood up to him when he was angry with me, sometimes putting herself in the line of fire to protect me. Despite this she never suggested that I consider divorce. When the time came that I realized I could not stay in the marriage, Ginna was there for me every day, providing love and support. She even became my roommate, so I did not have to live alone. In large and small ways, she helped me through the most painful experience of my life."

Loyalty may require making a judgment call, as in the case of Jennifer, a nurse, who spoke up when she felt that her friend was not being treated right by the man she was dating. She told us, "My best friend was in love with this guy I knew treated her very poorly. How do you talk to someone about that? For a while I didn't say anything, but after a time I started telling her, 'That's not fair'; 'You know he's not doing things that he should be doing for you'; 'He's ignoring you'; and so on. She defended him, but she didn't get mad at me, because she knew I was saying these things because I cared about her. Eventually they broke up, for which I was grateful. But then, to be loyal, I needed to support her while she grieved. I may not have liked the guy, but she had loved him for a long time. It's a hard balance, being angry at this guy but caring for

her at the same time. It was hard also because then she was upset and sad."

Loyalty also shows itself in choosing to spend time with our girlfriends. Bethany, a recent recipient of a master's degree, told us,

"I have a wonderful friend whom I only see when she travels to the West Coast on business. One time she flew in, and I told her I'd accommodate her business and social schedule. I knew she'd been invited out for a business dinner as well as to dinner with a male friend of hers. She told me, 'Absolutely not!' and she turned down these other invitations. She chose to spend time with me. She said, 'I want to come to your house for dinner and get into our robes and talk and talk.' To me, that feels like loyalty."

Many women have found that their girlfriends are there when no one else is, that the level of commitment remains constant no matter what else is going on in their lives. We may show loyalty to our friends by speaking up or merely showing up. Satiric author Fay Weldon offers her opinion of the value of her women friends in *Praxis:* "We shelter children for a time; we live side by side with men; and that is all. We owe them nothing and are owed nothing. I think we owe our friends more, especially our female friends."[1]

1. Fay Weldon, *Praxis* (New York: Penguin Books, 1990), 147.

Honesty

THE BEST MIND-ALTERING DRUG IS
TRUTH.
—*Lily Tomlin*

ONE MAY BE MY VERY GOOD FRIEND,
AND YET NOT OF MY OPINION.
—*Margaret Cavendish (1664)*

Being honest with one another is tough,
especially for many women. But every
woman needs a truth teller, and every relationship, in order to survive, requires that
truth be told. We all know the sadness of
friendships that fade because we can't bear

to reveal our true feelings. It is easy yet ultimately painful to let someone drift away because of unresolved conflict. The relationship in which truth is told is one that can be trusted, and every woman we interviewed felt that friendships that go through troubled times are strengthened by the test.

A girlfriend is one who can admit if she is upset with you and you can admit the same to her. Many of us raised as "good girls" fear conflict in a relationship because we do not realize that a real friendship can sustain conflict. Marilyn tells about Penny, a close girlfriend she's had for ten years. She said, "Penny came from a family where the expression of anger was not allowed. So, at the beginning of our relationship, I knew she was angry because she'd start acting weird, sort of withdrawn, not her usually enthusiastic self. I'd ask her if she was upset about something, and in a rush of emotion Penny would finally tell the truth about how she was feeling. After we sorted it all out, Penny would often tear up and say how surprised she was that our relationship could withstand anger. I told her that anger didn't scare me, but I was afraid of what would happen if she continued to hold in her feelings. As the years have gone by, Penny is much better about coming out with things right away, telling me she didn't like something I did or said. It gives me much more confidence in the future of our relationship now that she's willing to admit her feelings."

Some people may be afraid that they will

lose a friend if they express a negative opinion or feeling. Stories such as the one told by Faye, now in her fifties, about her friend

Eleanor, illustrate that friends can even argue without losing the friendship. "In twenty-five years of friendship, we have had two fights—one about four months ago. And it was a lulu. We fought while talking on the telephone, and it was over an oven, of all things. We both own the same horrendous piece of garbage that I unfortunately steered her to buy because I read about it. As it turns out, the fight wasn't about an oven at all but about the different ways we navigate life. We both had very personal ideas about what the outcome of this argument should be. We were isolated from each other because of our locked-in agenda. We were able to figure it out the following day."

Differences in individuals will invariably

lead to differences of opinion between them and may foster serious arguments, such as the one between Faye and Eleanor. We can defuse those arguments when we realize that differences of opinions are rarely about right or wrong; they are reflections of who we are as individuals. Friendships that mature beyond a bond of commonality to make room for differences are those strong enough to withstand the tests of time and change. And they give us what we all so desperately need—a safe, complete acceptance of who we are.

Good friends can also withstand our losing control of ourselves from time to time. Faye continued, "We love each other so much that we are almost over a fight by the next day. One fight I hung up on her. She never loses control; I do. I was livid. I screamed at her and hung up on her. That's the first time in twenty-five years." We asked her if she felt the friendship would end in one of those fights, and Faye responded, "Never, never, never, never, never. We're too important to each other."

Helen, a forty-six-year-old publicist, appreciates when someone has been honest with her, even though it was painful at the time: "I was involved in a five-year relationship with a very charismatic person who had a substance abuse problem. My father is an alcoholic, and I tended to be attracted to men who had that potential. This man was a tall, brooding poet, and he drove a cab and took cocaine to keep awake and to write late

at night, and of course nothing ever got edit-
ed or published. The relationship was bad,
and I was getting more and more involved
in his world. One night this man and I had a
party, and about halfway through the party
one of my friends—not even a very close
friend—said she wanted to talk to me. We
went into another room and shut the door,
and she just looked me right in the eye and
said, 'This is scary; he has a problem and
you have a problem and I really want you to
deal with this.' It was as if she had thrown
cold water in my face. I was shocked and
angry and just returned to the party.

"The next day we talked again, and about a
year and a half later violence occurred in the
relationship, and she was the one I went to at

midnight. I ended up staying at her house, and then I lived with her for a while. About a year and a half later I had to talk to her equally honestly about something that I saw her doing that I felt was unhealthy—an issue I felt she was skirting. She didn't like it either, but she had opened that honesty door between us. I think that took a lot of courage."

When a friendship is really strong, one friend may voice thoughts, feelings, or perspectives which the other may not be able to voice herself. It does, however, have its risks if the friend isn't receptive to what is being said. Donna, a forty-year-old marketing consultant, has had to face this risk. "I have a really good friend who has some emotional issues, and they get in the way of her really seeing her problems. So she keeps repeating the same thing over and over and over and making the same mistakes and clinging to the same fears. And our friendship will never progress past a certain point as a result of that. It takes courage and the ability to accept what other people are saying in order to have a real, full friendship." Friendship is limited when

we are not honest with our friends, but also, as Donna's relationship indicates, when we don't allow a friend to tell us what she perceives as the truth. We may not ultimately agree, but if our friend is trying to tell us something, perhaps we need to take some time to listen.

Stephanie Salter, columnist for the *San Francisco Examiner*, values her lifelong friends because "when you're telling them something, if it's bullshit, you can hear it in your own ears, because you know they know. They can keep you honest, the way I think visiting home again can keep you honest when you get the idea that who you are is totally independent of who you were." Honesty with a friend means speaking the truth with the intent of doing the best thing for the friend. However, honesty is not always about soul-searching issues. For instance, Susan told her close friend not to buy a certain dress, as she looked like Kermit the Frog. One of the author's friends says her glasses make her look like Tweety Bird. Girlfriends can tell you if your hair color is bad or if your boyfriend lied to you. The interesting thing is, so can your worst enemy. The difference is that your girlfriend does not relish it, and you just know that in your bones.

The Bonds of Humor

ONE CAN NEVER SPEAK ENOUGH
OF THE VIRTUES, THE DANGERS, THE
POWER OF SHARED LAUGHTER.

—*Françoise Sagan*

Many beautiful friendships arise and grow from a shared sense of humor. As Allison, a flower warehouse manager, avows, "My girlfriends and I have one rule: we can never go out with a guy or be friends with anyone who can't make us laugh. It's a good rule to follow."

Vanessa, sixteen, told us that Melissa has become one of her closest friends due to a shared sense of humor. "We became close friends on a camping trip with our church youth group. The first time we ever laughed together, just the two of us, it lasted for half an hour until we were gasping helplessly for air and clutching our aching stomachs. We were lying on the beach in California, giggling so hard we had sore muscles the next day. One of the things that amazes me about Melissa is that we both have the same twisted sense of humor. Many times we have been at a movie or watching a television show, and something that is not supposed to be humorous will have us rolling in the aisles. I have felt very alone without her, chortling at something and finding people staring. Together we are the essence of silliness. We sing silly songs, give huge bear hugs, make silly noises, and play silly games. This part of our friendship has saved us both from scary or sad situations. We have learned to deal with the aspects of our friendship that are in need of work or healing by balancing the seriousness with simple happiness."

Lest we believe that silliness is reserved for the young, Fern, a sixty-two-year-old Midwesterner, tells this story: "My friends Connie, Sandy, and I, when we were all in our thirties and forties, were together on a vacation in Florida (Connie had been ill and we were all tired of the cold winter weather, so we had decided to spend a few days in the sun). Connie had always been very reserved and discreet, with a Grace Kelly–like sophistication. At dinner one night, we started talking about the kinds of things we did for our husbands, whom we loved but who nevertheless could be exasperating. Suddenly a wry smile crept across Connie's face, as she

told us in great detail how her husband required twelve chocolate chips in each of his chocolate chip cookies and how she actually counted them out for each cookie. The image

of that devotion started all of us chortling. Then she went on to describe how she patiently (or not so patiently) reironed all his starched shirts from the laundry, because he didn't like the creases that the laundry left in them. She revealed that she had a mantra while performing this redundant chore: 'I love my husband, I love my husband, I love my husband' (through clenched teeth). We were roaring, laughing so hard we couldn't eat. Everyone at the restaurant was staring, although I could tell all of the women wanted to be at our table. We had such a wonderful evening; it provided a base for the layers of fun and enjoyment of the entire vacation."

Sometimes laughter is the only thing left to do and, quite possibly, the only thing that helps. Author Sue Monk Kidd tells this story of when her friend Betty was diagnosed with cancer: "Betty was in the hospital, having been told she would probably not live out the year. Everything was so serious and grim and heavy. She was lying there in bed with tubes coming out of nearly every available orifice, and I smiled at her and said, 'You know, you've got really bad hair.' Her hair was genuinely terrible. I mean, she hadn't washed it for weeks through all those surgeries. 'I know, it's horrible,' said Betty. I asked her if she wanted me to wash it. We weren't supposed to do that, of course. She was sick and there were those tubes and half a million stitches from surgery. But bad hair is

bad hair. Besides that, we had never been known for being sensible.

"Individually we might have been ordinary women but together we became Bette Midler, thumbing our noses at prudence. 'Yeah,' she said, 'wash it. Wash the stuff.' So I helped her get up, practically carried her and her entourage of tubes to the bathroom, and sat her on the side of the tub. Then I got the sprayer and began washing her hair. But the hose was unruly and she was soaked— her nightgown, everything. We stared at each other a minute, then burst into laughter.

"We laughed and laughed and laughed until the laughter took on a life of its own. We couldn't stop. And there was really something thrilling about that—for her to be laughing like this in the midst of all this angst and pain. I mean, my friend was facing death, and she was laughing her head off. She was living in the moment, finding whatever joy there was and wringing it out. That was ten years ago, and she is still going. Still laughing, still thumbing her nose at prudence."

Shared laughter offers us pleasure during the fun times and a resilient strength during distress. Sometimes life just seems too ridiculous and unexplainable. Laughing by yourself in these times seems somehow bitter and mirthless, but, as Sue and Betty discovered, laughter shared with a friend is sweet and healing.

Being There

I CAN TRUST MY FRIENDS. THESE PEOPLE FORCE ME TO EXAMINE, ENCOURAGE ME TO GROW.

—*Cher*

Many women say they appreciate their friends "being there" for them. We believe that "being there" requires the ability to empathize. One definition of empathy is "the capacity for participation in another's feelings or ideas."[2] The knowledge that the other person is accompanying us, is able to

2. *Webster's New Collegiate Dictionary.* (Springfield, MA: G. & C. Merriam Company, 1975), 373.

appreciate our feelings or ideas without necessarily agreeing with us, is powerful.

"Being there" also includes giving encouragement. We all need support, especially when we are exploring new talents or attempting a life change. Our friends can come to know our danger spots—the places where the bridge goes out most often—and help shore us up, give that extra oomph, the push, the clear-eyed reminder that we are doing the right thing. They also remind us when we are sliding from the path that is good for us or forgetting our value.

Anne, a forty-year-old entrepreneur, told us about her experience in starting up a new business with Chris, who is turning into a friend as well as a business associate. She

said, "We're out on a limb together with the chain saw running, but the relationship is more than that. As we go down this road, we're learning about each other—what we're frightened of, what we're good at, what we don't like to do. We're mutually supporting and helping and pushing each other. One will say, 'I can't do that yet,' and the other will say, 'Oh, yes, you can!' and so on. It's getting us through some very stressful and exciting days."

We believe that sometimes each of us is blessed with real empathy. Sometimes we can keep so still in our own mind, not focusing on our own agenda for our friend, that we can snatch a sense of what she truly needs. Sandra's friend, who was struggling to break out of an abusive relationship, probably kept coming to Sandra for empathy and encouragement because Sandra continued to recognize and acknowledge the steps she was taking to get out of the situation, no matter how subtle. When we have that intuitive connection with a friend, we know when she needs us to say, "You need to be doing more," and when you need to say, "That's really great that you took that little step."

Sue told us about how she encouraged her friend Betty after Betty was diagnosed with terminal cancer. Sue said, "I remember sitting in the hospital room holding hands while she said, 'I will not die!' with me repeating back to her, 'You will not die.' She is still alive, ten years later, but we went through years of not knowing whether she would live or not.

"A lot of things that we feel helped save Betty's life were things we did together, unconventional things that we'd never done

before. Betty felt she'd boxed herself into a
very tight, conventional way of life and had
not allowed her female self any freedom. It
was true of me too. So we would go out to
the woods and dance or dress up in wild
hats with ostrich feathers in them and wear
outlandish outfits. We'd pretend to be the
Bette Midler character in the movie *Beaches*,
that outlandish, free, feisty broad that Betty
needed and I needed, too. We would dare
one another; that was part of our relationship. It was outlandish and wild and wonderful, and we laughed and laughed. It was
really important."

Mary, in her mid-thirties, tells of her friend
Susan, who encourages and inspires her, even
when Susan is the one suffering. Mary told us,

"When Susan's child Aaron was born in 1990 with an open laceration to his brain, she and her husband were informed that he had a chromosome disorder, Trisomy-13, with a terminal prognosis. Aaron should already be dead according to all the experts. Although his survival is miraculous, Aaron's needs are constant, and the emotional and financial drain on my friend concerns me the most. Susan has reached great heights of courage. She is a true hero. When her mind is sore, heart empty, and her body exhausted, I can hear her soul whispering clearly, 'Keep living, loving, and laughing.' All I can do is offer Susan a hug, an ear, and time; I am her girlfriend.

"Even with this burden on her shoulders, she has taken time to give me another gift: She has taught me not to fear the handicapped. I spent most of my life running from the handicapped, afraid to touch them because 'If I touch you, I will be like you.' I could not appreciate minds that were of lesser intelli-

gence than mine. As Susan learned about her gifted child, so did I. She would share books and literature and invite me to support group seminars, and slowly my fears were healed."

50

"Being there" includes both empathy, the willingness to put ourselves in our friend's place, and the offering of encouragement when our friend's supply of faith is low. Sometimes, as in Mary and Susan and Betty and Sue's cases, the encouragement we give our friends is reciprocated simultaneously. Mary gave support to Susan while Susan encouraged Mary to accept a handicapped child. Sue shared her faith, and Betty helped assuage Sue's fear of Betty's death. Shared encouragement and empathy can propel us further than we would ever be able to go if left on our own. Sometimes there is no greater gift we can give each other than simply "being there."

Strength

À COEUR VAILLANT RIEN
D'IMPOSSIBLE.
NOTHING IS IMPOSSIBLE TO A
VALIANT HEART.
—*Jeanne d'Albret*
(motto adopted by her son
Henry IV) c. 1550

Almost everyone we talked to said she loved
Little Women as a girl, either the book or the
movie. Anna Quindlen, in her *New York
Times* column of April 29, 1990, said she had
done an informal survey among the men
and women she knew, and not one of the

men knew who Jo March was: "One guessed that Jo March was a second baseman for the Baltimore Orioles."[3] On the other hand, every woman she talked to answered the question correctly. Why do so many of us identify with Jo? Anna Quindlen's theory is: "Jo is the smart one, and that is why she left an indelible mark. She showed that there was more to life than spinning skeins into gold and marrying a prince." However, there is another aspect of Jo that impresses us—she is also the strong one.

At certain times in our lives, we need to rely on the strength of our friends. Sue

3. Anna Quindlen, "Heroine Addiction," in *Thinking Out Loud: On the Personal, the Political, the Public, and the Private* (New York: Ballantine/Fawcett, 1993), 267.

Bender, author of *Plain and Simple,* credits
her friendship with Mitzi McClosky, a thera-
pist, with giving her the courage to give
birth to her book. "Without Mitzi and our
conversations, I never could have done it.
We met informally once a week, a meeting
that for me became a sacred ritual. She is my
beloved friend, somebody who tells the
truth and reflects back on things."

Sue told us she was very grateful for
Mitzi's support but for some time felt uncer-
tain as to what she was giving in exchange.
Several years later, their roles reversed, and
their relationship now illustrates the miracle
of friendship—how we trade roles and
exchange gifts. Mitzi described herself as
becoming "obsessed" with the problems and

issues connected with caregiving for elderly parents and began keeping notes and writing thoughts on the subject on the backs of envelopes and in her journal. Sue encouraged her to put all her jottings into a book. As Mitzi explains, "Thanks to Sue's prompting, I arranged the material and began to type it up. I now have a complete manuscript: *Mollie's Golden Years.* Sue's and my roles have reversed. Sue has read what I've written, and I think she wrote the most eloquent criticism—thoughtful and honest—that I have ever seen. Receiving help had always been difficult for me. Sue taught me how to accept a gift with generosity of spirit. From her I learned that receiving can be a gift to the giver."

Women also gain strength in groups; packs of women can get more accomplished than one woman by herself. And working in a group can give us the courage and momentum to step in where we wouldn't necessarily have done so alone. Martha, now a homemaker in Pennsylvania, found that she and her friends could accomplish a great deal together: "When I worked as an administrative manager for a large company, three other women in approximately equivalent positions and I got in the habit of meeting for coffee breaks and sometimes lunch together. We shared our frustrations and sympathized with one another.

"Just before Christmas, one woman found out that one of her employees had been evicted and would be living in her car with her son and pregnant daughter. We organized a fund-raising drive and in three days raised first, last, and deposit rent payments. We celebrated by having dinner together and drinking Pink Ladies. We became 'The Pink Ladies,' and each had a club name

(Scarlett, Wonder Woman, BonBon, and Miss Feathers). We had regular dinners after that, and ten years later, all working for different companies—and me having moved away—we still stay in touch and meet when we can."

Women who have banded together not only get a lot done; they also gather a surprising amount of power. Sandra Martz, founder of Papier-Mache Press and editor of *When I Am an Old Woman I Shall Wear Purple,* told us this story of a group of friends that formed over twenty years ago: "In the early seventies, I was working for a large corporation in a clerical job. This was about the time that the women's movement reared its head. The corporation I worked for was a government contractor and under the review of the Equal Employment Opportunity Commission, which audited companies on issues of equality in the workplace. At the same time, there was a lot of grass roots organizing on the part of women in the company. Some of these women began to get involved in company-sponsored affirmative action programs and special committees. There was a particular committee composed of all women, of which I eventually became a member, that acted as an advisory group to top management. After a while, we began to feel that management was using the group to placate the EEOC officers when they came in. We felt that management was pointing to us and saying, 'We're really doing great. Look how

we've got this group of women who identi-
fies women's concerns, and we respond to
their needs.' In reality, many of the big issues
that the group identified, such as child care

and putting women into management roles, were never addressed.

"Our feelings culminated in what we perceived as a very radical act, which was to disband the committee. We all got together in someone's living room and signed a letter of resignation, saying, 'We're not going to be your vehicle anymore,' and presented it to the head of the company. It was really exciting and felt very radical. This act of defiance cemented the bonds that had already started forming and left the women feeling part of something very important. At the same time, however, it removed one of the formal vehicles that we had for getting together. In an almost spontaneous way, a smaller group of the women began meeting weekly for lunch.

"We got together and simply began to share information. For instance, a woman working in one of the business offices would tell us about budget cuts that were coming or new organizations that were being formed. If one woman was having a problem, the others would share from their own experiences about what to do or who to see. Some of the conversation was just rowdy and raucous. The group decided to call itself SLUG. The S was never defined, but the LUG was Ladies Underground. We'd use this name to send out information to each other. The men in the organization were incredibly curious and anxious, and sometimes terrified, especially those higher up in the organization or in personnel or human relations. There was virtually no part of the company that we didn't have covered. And we were perceived as this radical group who had pissed off top management. It was great fun. We loved it. Over time our group became very close and developed into a social group as well. It was a powerful support group, because we all knew and understood the work environment we were in and had also known each other long enough to have a sense of one another's personal situations. There was simply unconditional support among us, even though we were all quite different. As a result of this support and SLUG, the careers of the women in this group thrived. It was incredible."

There are women in our lives who are like Jo in *Little Women*. Sometimes she is one

64

woman alone, sometimes a group. Jo was good-hearted, but not afraid to step in a little mud. And

that is what we learn to respect in our girl-friends. They are strong when things are really messy, when we are snarling, raging, or mourning, when we are finding new courage in ourselves. They stride right into the muck and take the situation in hand. Sometimes it is the intensity of the muck that really establishes the friendship. All we may need is one friend to share her strength, and we can become clearheaded and courageous again.

Being Heard

IF YOU WANT TO BE LISTENED TO, YOU
SHOULD PUT IN TIME LISTENING.
—*Marge Piercy*

THERE WAS NO WAY FOR ME TO UNDER-
STAND IT AT THE TIME, BUT THE TALK
THAT FILLED THE KITCHEN THOSE AFTER-
NOONS WAS HIGHLY FUNCTIONAL. IT
SERVED AS THERAPY, THE CHEAPEST KIND
AVAILABLE TO MY MOTHER AND HER
FRIENDS. . . . BUT MORE THAN THERAPY,
THAT FREEWHEELING, WIDE-RANGING,
EXUBERANT TALK FUNCTIONED AS AN
OUTLET FOR THE TREMENDOUS CREATIVE
ENERGY THEY POSSESSED.
—*Paule Marshall*

Miraculously, our most serious situations seem to lighten when we tell them to a friend and feel that she has heard us. The magic happens when a friend is able to put herself in our place and, knowing us as she does, can help us come to a decision without necessarily solving the problem for us. Being heard is a clarifying potion—not made by any cosmetics company—that helps us to see things clearly. Cheryl, a teacher and mother of two, commented, "Until you've actually bounced an idea off another friend, you can't clarify it in your mind."

Tamara, one of the authors, described it this way: "I tend to see problems as two-dimensional—huge, flat movie-screen images coming at me. I think I see a problem and then I feel that the problem must be my fault somehow, so there is this added sense of shame or guilt around the situation. It is overwhelming. I can escape from this downward spiral in an emotional emergency by calling all my friends and talking over the problem.

Just the fact that I am saying it out loud to each of them helps me view the situation more realistically. And their responses each add a level of perspective and wisdom that allows me to see a different view of the

problem. The problem, whatever it is, becomes life-size instead of larger than life, and I start seeing it in perspective. It makes the problem three-dimensional, if you will, and therefore deflatable."

Suzy, a poet now living in suburban Connecticut, underscores the importance of having a good friend listen to us with this story: "At one point in my life, I married a former boyfriend who lived on the West Coast. I left New York and a middle-class life to become a hippie, living with Jon on a commune in the remote woods of northern California with no phone and no electricity. Karen and I started corresponding. Those letters, the slower process of reflection and writing, created another level of intimacy between us. I would write to her during those two A.M. hours of insomnia when marital or work anxiety beset me. Sometimes I wouldn't mail them, although I started each letter 'Dear Karen' with her eyes and ears as

the intended audience. Somehow, just thinking she might read what I was writing
calmed me. After I'd poured out my feelings
on paper, I'd feel able to return to bed."

The necessity of having a listening friend
is illustrated by Anne Frank's story. Anne,
locked in her hideaway, did not have a girlfriend, so she made one up, her diary. As
Patricia Hampl wrote about the new defini-
tive edition of the diary released in spring of
1995, "From the first, she addressed the
notebook as a trusted girlfriend: 'I'll begin
from the moment I got you, the moment I
saw you lying on the table among my other
birthday presents.' A few days later this
anonymous 'you' becomes the imaginary
'Kitty,' and the entries turn into letters, giv-

ing the diary the intimacy and vivacity of a developing friendship."[4]

Clarity and perspective are what we gain from our friends who hear us, really hear us, who take the time to stop other tasks and focus on what we are saying. How powerful that act is, and how powerfully even imagining a friend listening, as Anne Frank and Suzy did, can affect us. High-quality listening, even more than high-quality advice, can keep us grounded and help us listen to our own hearts, finding our answers within ourselves.

4. Patricia Hampl, "The Whole Anne Frank," *The New York Times Book Review*, March 5, 1995, 1, 21.

Saving Our Lives

DOES THAT MEAN I NEVER LET HER
DOWN? DOES THAT MEAN THE RHYTHM
IS ALWAYS IN STEP? IT MEANS THAT IN
SPITE OF OR INCLUDING THESE ISSUES, I
ABSOLUTELY CAN COUNT ON HER. AND
WHAT IS SO VALUABLE IS THAT I DON'T
BELIEVE THAT IS OPEN TO QUESTION.

—*Catherine Smith, Ph.D.*

We have heard many stories about girlfriends
saving each other's lives, most often figura-
tively and sometimes literally. Anne, a child-
hood educator now retired, tells this story
about how a friend helped her in her career:

"I was studying at the University of Iowa and was finishing up my master's thesis. I was getting ready to move to the East Coast, and although I had finished my course work and written the thesis, I was running out of time before I moved, and the thesis needed to be typed. I knew I would not finish it once I was out of the school environment, because I just knew I would become distracted. I don't ever remember asking her for help, but my friend

Carolyn showed up—she was an excellent typist—and typed my thesis. If she hadn't typed it, I would not have finished my master's degree. That act of friendship has made a big difference in my life, as the master's degree opened doors that would not have opened without it."

Elizabeth, thirty-five, told us another story about receiving the help she needed without having to ask. "Kim called one morning a few years ago, just to check in. When one of my children answered and said, 'Mommy's sick,' Kim immediately got in her car, drove over, and picked up and kept my three small children for the day. I was too sick even to argue, and she knew it."

Roberta, a secretary in her thirties, tells this

story: "When I attempted suicide and came out of it, the first person I saw was Colleen, crying. I asked her why she was crying, and she said something like, 'Because you're here in the hospital.' I don't recall anyone else being there; I'm sure they were around, but not when I became conscious. Colleen is really great, very strong and supportive, discreet and very diplomatic, and for her to cry really means she cared a lot whether or not I lived. She is not very emotionally forthright—I don't think she ever cried in front of me when her grandmother or father died—so her emotion meant a lot to me. Suddenly I understood that what I did had had an effect on her. Up until then I was just thinking how I would like to leave the plan-

et, not really thinking of the consequences for family and friends around me."

Asked how she thought Colleen's presence helped her get through that difficult time in her life, Roberta replied, "Colleen was a really good friend to me. It was hard for me to explain why I was so depressed, but she would never push for answers, explanations. She just helped me by listening, always without judgment and criticism. And she would always be there to take me to the doctor, to listen for hours on the phone, and so forth. I must have been a pain in the neck."

Sometimes we are rescued by our friends just staying with us, as we swirl around in a crisis or tiptoe over a slick, glassy place in our lives. The following story, which Sue told, provides the perfect metaphor for so many of the situations in which our friends save our lives. Sue, an author, began: "Betty and I were having a picnic by a river, and I had this bright idea that we should walk across the river to the other side. So we took our shoes off and tied them together, threw them over our shoulders, rolled up our pants, and started across. I went first and got about halfway when I realized the currents were stronger than they looked. I lost my balance somewhat and my shoes fell off my shoulders. I thought: I'm going to get those shoes, they cost eighty dollars.

"So I went after the shoes, and Betty was still on the bank. I was taken by the current and getting in over my head fast—literally. I real-

ized about forty yards downriver that I may not get those shoes. In fact, perhaps I wouldn't get out myself! Betty was running as fast as she could along the riverbank with me, somehow managing to keep up. She stayed with me every bit of the way, saying, 'I'm with you, I'm with you. Hang in there, I'll get you!'

"She found a long branch, which I finally grabbed and got out. But I'll always remember her running along, saying, 'I'm with you.' That captures something about unconditional love between women. It's an enduring tie we know we have."

Acknowledgments

Many thanks to those who contributed photographs:

Judy Abbate
Julie Herman
Beth Hood
Margaret Hood
JuJu Johnson
Susan Miller
Dorothy O'Brien
Leola Specht
Leslie Watkins

. No batteries to buy — She's

8. Environmentally friendly a
   litter or harmful fumes.

7. Get to live out secret fant
   Sprout to her Jolly Green

6. Does not promote tooth de

5. Five flight walk-up fulfills
   to get more exercise.

4. Her soothing reassurances
   happen to Bush.

3. Two words: FREE FOOD

2. Her decorating advice less costl
   to _4,001 Home Ideas_

1. I love her!